leatherback turtle

green turtle

loggerhead turtle

1 They go on amazing journeys

Steering gracefully with their flippers, sea turtles look like they are flying underwater. They swim thousands of miles between their feeding and nesting places.

green turtle

deep ocean

bottlenose dolphin

They cross huge oceans, mysteriously returning to nest on the beach where they were born. Nobody is quite sure how they find their way.

school of sardines

reef shark

② They cry real tears

Sea turtles only drink seawater, so their bodies get very salty. Too much salt is bad for them, so turtles get rid of it by shedding big, salty tears.

green turtle

eye

tears

flipper

shell

tail

On land, crying also helps to flush gritty sand out of their eyes. They cry underwater too, but the sea washes their tears away.

3 Their nests save sand dunes

Leaving tire-like tracks behind them, female turtles crawl up the beach to nest. Some nest alone, but others nest in big groups. They each dig a deep hole and lay a slippery pile of eggs.

nest

eggs

olive ridley turtle

SHOW YOU LOVE A TURTLE

Don't disturb nesting turtles! If you are on a turtle beach, give them space to nest and hatch.

sand dunes

grasses

tracks

The eggs hatch, leaving hundreds of broken shells. These provide food for grasses growing in the dunes. The grass roots stop the wind from blowing away the sand, keeping the dunes in place.

seagull

ghost crab

4 They race for the sea

Baby sea turtles hatch together at night. They dig themselves out of their sandy holes and scramble toward the sparkling moonlit waters of the sea.

starfish

hatchlings

waves

Bright lights tempt some away from the water. Others are snatched by gulls and crabs as they run down the beach. The lucky ones swim frantically into the breaking waves.

5 Their jaws snip and snap

The shape of turtle jaws depends on what they eat. Some have scissor-like jaws to snatch drifting jellyfish. Others have sharp "beaks" to poke into rocky crevices and coral reefs for shellfish and crabs. And some have jagged jaws to snip sea grass.

comb jellyfish

pink helmet jellyfish

moon jellyfish

lion's mane jellyfish

plastic bag

leatherback turtle

SHOW YOU LOVE A TURTLE

Don't leave litter on the beach! Plastic bags can wash into the sea, where turtles gobble them up by mistake.

6 They are deep-sea gardeners

In shallow, sunny waters, sea turtles act like underwater lawn mowers. By nibbling sea grass meadows to keep them short and healthy, turtles make homes for millions of fish, crabs, and even sea horses.

hawksbill turtle

coral

sponge

They graze these busy underwater gardens for up to three hours, before popping up for air.

SHOW YOU LOVE A TURTLE

Learn about climate change! It's destroying coral reefs, which are dying as the sea warms up.

sea horse

green turtle

lobster

7 They hold their breath for hours

Like us, sea turtles need air, so they poke their heads above water to breathe. But they can also take one huge breath that lasts for hours when they are diving or sleeping underwater.

loggerhead turtle

Pacific gull

flying fish

fishing boat

7806

net

SHOW YOU LOVE A TURTLE

Eat responsibly caught fish! Turtles drown if they get tangled up in fishing nets.

They are as ancient as the dinosaurs

Turtles have been on Earth for millions of years. They once walked on land around the feet of dinosaurs. These early turtles were twice the size of sea turtles today and had much longer necks.

dragonfly

pterodactyl

stegosaurus

ferns

Perhaps these ancient turtles first slid into water to look for food. Today, all turtles live in the ocean and only struggle back onto land to lay their eggs.

diplodocus

ancient turtle

9 They have beautiful shells

Most animals with shells can pull their head and legs inside them for protection. But sea turtle shells are different...

leatherback

Their shells are part of their backs, so their flippers and head always stick out.

SHOW YOU LOVE A TURTLE

Don't buy anything made from turtle shell! Sea turtle shells are made into jewelry and other tourist souvenirs.

olive ridley

These beautiful, patterned
shells protect their bodies
from predators like sharks and
crocodiles.

hawksbill

green turtle

10 They grow very old

These quiet, gentle creatures grow very slowly and live a long time. Some survive for 150 years—much longer than us! But in oceans around the world, these ancient reptiles are being killed by pollution, hunting, and fishing. They are disappearing fast.

Kemp's ridley

olive ridley

leatherback